LANDSCAPES OF LIGHT

Photographs by

Robert Cooper

An Illustrated Anthology
of Prayers

David Adam

First published in Great Britain in 2001 by
Society for Promoting Christian Knowledge
Holy Trinity Church
Marylebone Road
London NW1 4DU

British Library Cataloguing-in-Publication Data
A catalogue record for this book is available from the British Library

ISBN 0-281-05320-0

5   7   9   10   8   6   4

Designed and typeset by Alison Guy
Printed in Singapore by KWF Printing Pte Ltd

FOREWORD

God created the world out of love, out of the glory and beauty of His own being. Everything in the world has the potential of revealing His glory. If we do not behold His glory, it is because we have not looked deep enough or close enough at what is about us. There is always a great danger of becoming insensitive to the world in which we live. Sometimes we do not notice because we do not stop long enough to give our attention to what is there waiting to be seen. We must remember that vision is about seeing. Visionaries are those who see further or deeper than the majority, but we are all capable of vision and extending our vision.

Every now and then, someone comes along who extends our vision and helps us to become more aware of what is about us. Poets, artists, musicians and photographers all help us to extend our awareness. Robert Cooper, who has taken all the photographs in this book, is such a person. Robert has an eye that sees: he is aware of the deep down mystery and beauty that is waiting to be revealed in the ordinary. The photographs in this book can be seen as meditations, each image can be used to awaken and extend our own vision of what is about us. Perhaps they will lead us to discover, as St Patrick said:

> Our God is a God of all,
> God of heaven and earth, seas and rivers,
> God of sun and moon, and all the stars,
> God of high mountains and of lowly valleys,
> God over heaven, and in heaven and under heaven,
> He has His dwelling
> In heaven and earth and sea, and all things that are in them.

DAVID ADAM

RISING PRAYER

Thanks be to the Father
I arise today
He gives me light
He guides my way

Thanks be to the Saviour
I arise today
He gives me love
He hears me pray

Thanks be to the Spirit
I arise today
He gives me life
With me to stay

CREATOR OF LIGHT

Creator of light
The blessing of light be upon us
The blessing of daylight
The blessing of sunlight
The blessing of Christ light
Scatter the darkness from before us
That we may walk as children of light

WAKEN ME, O LORD

Waken me, O Lord
    Open my eyes to your glory
    Open my ears to your story
    Open my heart to your fire
    Open my will to your desire

Waken me, O Lord
    To your risen power
    To your Presence every hour
    To your never-ending love
    To your coming from above

Waken me, O Lord
    To your peace here today
    To your meeting in the way
    To your speaking in a friend
    To your guiding to the end

Waken me, O Lord, to your glory

Where the mist rises from the sea
Where the waves creep upon the shore
Where the wrack lifts upon the strand
            I have seen the Lord

Where the sun awakens the day
Where the road winds on its way
Where the fields are sweet with hay
            I have seen the Lord

Where the stars shine in the sky
Where the streets so peaceful lie
Where the darkness is so nigh
            I have seen the Lord

The Lord is here
The Lord is there
The Lord is everywhere
The Lord is high
The Lord is low
The Lord is on the path I go

I HAVE SEEN THE LORD

THOU ART GOD

Thou art the peace of all things calm

Thou art the place to hide from harm

Thou art the light that shines in dark

Thou art the heart's eternal spark

Thou art the door that's open wide

Thou art the guest who waits inside

Thou art the stranger at the door

Thou art the calling of the poor

Thou art my Lord and with me still

Thou art my love, keep me from ill

Thou art my light, the truth, the way

Thou art my Saviour this very day

GOD BLESS
THE EARTH

God bless the earth
And all living creatures
God bless the earth
With its rugged features
God bless the earth
Every town and city
God bless the earth
With all its industry
God bless the earth
Atmosphere and air
God bless the earth
Keep it in your care
God bless the earth
Protect the living soil
God bless the earth
May nothing despoil
God bless the earth
And its daily light
God bless the earth
Preserve it by your might

BEFORE
PRAYER

I weave a silence on to my lips
I weave a silence into my mind
I weave a silence within my heart
I close my ears to distractions
I close my eyes to attractions
I close my heart to temptations

Calm me O Lord, as you stilled the storm
Still me O Lord, keep me from harm
Let all the tumult within me cease
Enfold me Lord in your peace

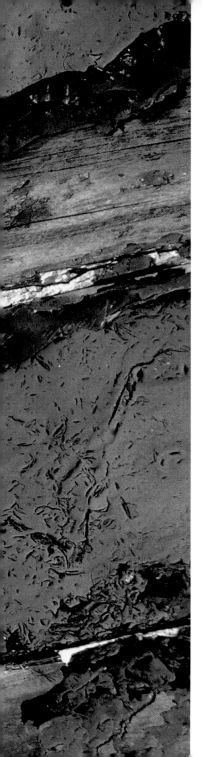

OPENINGS

O Lord God, Creator of all

Open my eyes to beauty

Open my mind to wonder

Open my ears to others

Open my heart to you

GOD OF THE ELEMENTS

God of the elements, glory to you

Glory to you for flowing air

Glory for light beyond compare

Glory for water as it flows

Glory for soil and all that grows

Glory for life and love and birth

Glory to you, Lord of the earth

HELP ME, LORD

Help me, Lord, to see
You are about me
You are my hope

In my lying down and rising
In my travelling and arriving
    Help me, Lord, to see
    You are about me
    You are my hope

In my sorrow and enjoyment
In my work and unemployment
    Help me, Lord, to see
    You are about me
    You are my hope

In my peacefulness and strife
In my going from this life
    Help me, Lord, to see
    You are about me
    You are my hope

In my achievement and its waning
In my losing or my gaining
    Help me, Lord, to see
    You are about me
    You are my hope

CIRCLE ME, LORD

Circle me, Lord
Keep protection near
And danger afar

Circle me, Lord
Keep hope within
Keep doubt without

Circle me, Lord
Keep light near
And darkness afar

Circle me, Lord
Keep peace within
Keep evil out

POWER TO WORK

Lord you are
The love of my life
The light of my way
The peace of my mind
The power for my task
The Presence

Help me
Strong One
To be a strength to the weak
Help me
Caring One
To be a support to the sad
Help me
Saving One
To be a helper of the lost
Help me
Present One
To be a comfort to the lonely
Help me
Holy One
To worship you now and evermore

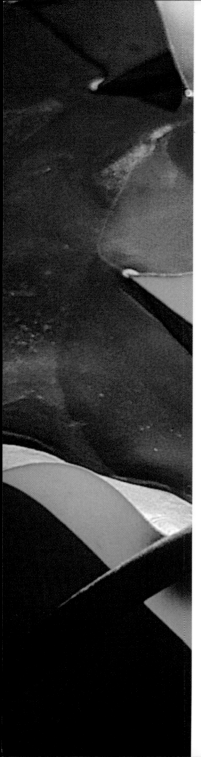

VISION

O Lord

Extend our vision

Our clearness of sight

Open our eyes to see

Beyond the obvious

To perceive that this is your world

You are in it

You invade it

You pervade it

You enfold it

It is immersed in you

LIGHT OF THE WORLD

Light of the world
Enter into the depths
of our lives

Come into the dark
and hidden places

Walk in the storehouse
of our memories

Hear the hidden secrets
of the past

Plumb the very depth
of our being

Be present through
the silent hours

And bring us safely
to your glorious light

ADORATION

Father,
>In you is my birth
>In you is the earth
>In you is eternal worth
>>I bow before you

Jesus,
>In you is love so dear
>In you salvation near
>In you I lose my fear
>>I bow before you

Spirit,
>In you is all strong power
>In you is every hour
>In you my life will flower
>>I bow before you

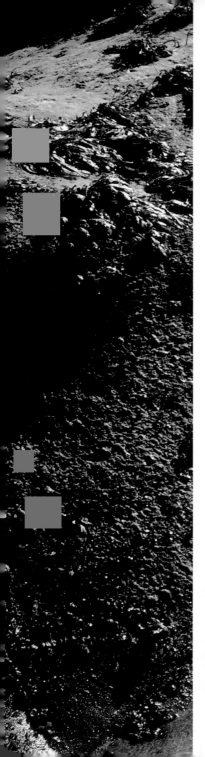

INVOCATION

On all of creation

The animate and inanimate

The weak and the strong

The young and the old

The wise and the simple

The free and the captive

The peaceful and the anxious

The joyful and the sad

The saint and the sinner

The living and the dead

Be the grace and glory of God

UNTIL THE TIDE TURNS

Lord,
I wait for the tide to turn
Until the distant becomes close
Until the far off becomes near
Until the outside is within
Until the ebb flows

Lord,
I wait for the tide to turn
Until weakness is made strong
Until blindness turns to sight
Until the fractured is made whole
Until the ebb flows

Lord,
I wait until the tide turns
Until the ordinary becomes strange
Until the empty is Presence-full
Until the two become one
Until the ebb flows

BY THE ROWAN

By the rowan and the briar

By the raging forest fire

By the sky in lightning torn

By the moon that's newly born

By the rising of the sun

By the task that I have done

I bind my feeble soul to thee

Almighty, Son and Spirit Three

JESUS, YOU ARE THE LIGHT OF THE WORLD

Jesus, you are the light of the world
A light that no darkness can quench

Upon your church
Wrestling with the darkness of evil
Battling against doubt
Let your light shine

Upon the world governments
Facing gloom and despair
Battling against disaster
Let your light shine

Upon those that live in the shadows
Caught up in sorrow and strife
Struggling against oblivion
Let your light shine

THE GATE OF GLORY

Lord,
   When our steps are weary
   And the going is rough
   When our life is dreary
   And our journey is tough
            Open the gate of glory

Lord,
   When the dark clouds thicken
   And the storm rides high
   When the troubles quicken
   And danger is nigh
            Open the gate of glory

Lord,
   When our work is completed
   And the battle is done
   We are not defeated
   The victory you have won
            Open the gate of glory

TO ETERNITY

Where does the journey end?
Beyond where you can see

Where do the years end?
That's unknown to you or me

Where does life end?
In love and eternity

SEEING IN A NEW LIGHT

Light is the photographer's medium. It is also a metaphor of revelation – we speak of illumination and enlightenment. When T. S. Eliot described light as 'investing form with lucid stillness/Turning shadow into transient beauty',[1] he was writing as a photographer sees. The photographer's awareness is tuned constantly to changes in the angle, direction, colour and intensity of light. Compared with painting, this momentary art – measured in the clicking shutter's hundredths, even thousandths of a second – is sometimes seen as shallow. Ironically, the camera, which proverbially never lies, is deemed unable to enlighten – to tell the deepest truth. Yet this is to misunderstand the process. Its very transience is an advantage, because it leads to an intense awareness of the present moment and of the value of passing things.

Of all the images in this book, the one that best expresses my own vision is of the kelp. Normally, it just floats there, dull and flabby, but against the sun's rays it shines gold. It is transfigured – as are people when they are seen through the lens of God's mercy and love, with all their potential and infinite possibilities. Just as in nature, despite all that has been done to pollute it, there remains the 'dearest freshness deep down things',[2] so there is a beauty to be discovered in people once the layers of prejudice and false perception are peeled away. Photography can transfigure people and things by revealing them 'in a new light'. Through the lens all things potentially become a source of wonder. All things – even when they are not obviously beautiful.

Much of Holy Island, where these pictures were taken, is bare and uninviting. When the wind blows – and it often does – it can cut to the bone. For all the ravishing beauty of the dawn and the bewitching sparkle of the surrounding sea, being on the island is not always a cosy experience. Yet God is as present in the mists of uncertainty, the chill winds of suffering, the apparently insignificant or the cast aside, as in the glory of the dawn. It is this conviction that these photographs attempt to share.

ROBERT COOPER

---

[1] T. S. Eliot, 'Burnt Norton', in *Four Quartets*, Faber and Faber, 1944, lines 93–4, p. 17.

[2] Gerard Manley Hopkins, 'God's Grandeur', in *Poems and Prose*, Harmondsworth Penguin, 1953, p.27.

REFERENCES

Prayers are drawn from four of David Adam's books: *The Edge of Glory* (EG), *Tides and Seasons* (TS), *Power Lines* (PL) and *The Open Gate* (OG), all published by Triangle, London.

Photographs and prayers in order of appearance:

Cover: St Cuthbert's Island, early morning
Putting to sea, early morning, 'Rising Prayer' (*TS*, p. 8).
Sands at low tide, 'Creator of Light' (*OG*, p. 28).
Dawn light, 'Waken Me, O Lord' (*PL*, p. 4).
The village from the harbour, early morning, 'I Have Seen the Lord' (*TS*, p. 28).
The Priory ruins, seen from St Cuthbert's Island, 'Thou art God' (*EG*, p. 13).
The old staithes, 'God Bless the Earth' (*PL*, p. 39).
Reflections in the Ouse, early morning, 'Before Prayer' (*EG*, p. 7).
Peeling paint, 'Openings' (*PL*, p. 9).
Dawn light on St Cuthbert's Island, 'God of the Elements' (*OG*, p. 88).
The Pilgrims' Way, 'Help Me, Lord' (*PL*, p. 6).
Stone, marked by the waves, 'Circle Me, Lord' (*EG*, p. 8).
Statue of St Aidan, 'Power to Work' (*PL*, p. 23).
Kelp – turned golden by the light, 'Vision' (*PL*, p. 27).
Looking towards the mainland, evening, 'Light of the World' (*PL*, p. 71).
Flower on Cockle Stone beach, 'Adoration' (*PL*, p. 10).
At Castlehead Rocks, 'Invocation' (*PL*, p. 40).
Sands near the causeway, 'Until the Tide Turns' (*TS*, p. 96).
Autumn berries, 'By the Rowan' (*EG*, p. 36).
Navigation marker, 'Jesus, You are the Light of the World' (*OG*, p. 55).
Looking towards the Cheviot Hills over St Cuthbert's Island, 'The Gate of Glory' (*TS*, p. 129).
The Pilgrims' Way at sunset, 'To Eternity' (*TS*, p. 117).